W9-BPJ-944

FIRST PEOPLES

THE MASAI

OF AFRICA

LISA McQUAIL

Lerner Publications Company • Minneapolis

**First American edition published in 2002
by Lerner Publications Company**

Published by arrangement with Times Editions
Copyright © 2002 by Times Media Private Limited

Lerner Publications Company
A division of Lerner Publishing Group
241 First Avenue North
Minneapolis, MN 55401 U.S.A.
Website address: www.lernerbooks.com

Series originated and designed by
Times Editions
An imprint of Times Media Private Limited
A member of the Times Publishing Group
1 New Industrial Road, Singapore 536196
Website address: www.timesone.com.sg/te

Series editors: Margaret J. Goldstein, Daphne Rodrigues
Series designers: Tuck Loong, Jailani Basari
Series picture researcher: Susan Jane Manuel

Library of Congress Cataloging-in-Publication Data
McQuail, Lisa, 1960-
The Masai of Africa / by Lisa McQuail.— 1st American ed.
p. cm. — (First peoples)
Includes bibliographical references and index.
ISBN 0-8225-4855-0 (lib. bdg. : alk. paper)
1. Masai (African people)—History—Juvenile literature. 2. Masai (African
people)—Social life and customs—Juvenile literature. 3. Kenya—Description
and travel—Juvenile literature. 4. Tanzania—Description and travel—Juvenile
literature. [1. Masai (African people) 2. Africa, East.] I. Title. II. Series.
DT433.545.M33 M36 2002
967.6'004965—dc21   2001000848

Printed in Singapore
Bound in the United States of America

1 2 3 4 5 6—0S—07 06 05 04 03 02

CONTENTS

WHO ARE THE MASAI?

The Masai are a group of native people who live in the countries of Kenya and Tanzania in East Africa. The Masai number more than 377,000. They have lived in East Africa for hundreds of years, and their lifestyle has changed very little. Early explorers described the Masai as fierce warriors but also admired their physical beauty. Both the men and women are tall and slim, with dark, smooth skin. They paint their bodies and faces and wear colorful beaded jewelry and cloaks made from animal skins.

A Bountiful Land

The Masai live in southern Kenya and northern Tanzania. This region is called Masailand. It has wide open grassy plains, large lakes and long winding rivers, towering snowcapped mountains, and a variety of plants and animals found in few other places on earth.

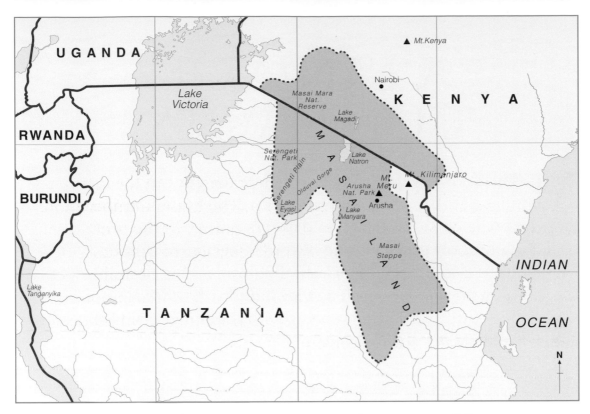

Map labels:
UGANDA
RWANDA
BURUNDI
TANZANIA
KENYA
Lake Victoria
Lake Tanganyika
Lake Eyasi
Lake Manyara
Lake Natron
Lake Magadi
Serengeti Nat. Park
Serengeti Plain
Olduvai Gorge
Masai Mara Nat. Reserve
Arusha Nat. Park
Masai Steppe
MASAILAND
Nairobi
Arusha
▲ Mt. Kenya
▲ Mt. Meru
▲ Mt. Kilimanjaro
INDIAN OCEAN
N

Wandering Warriors in a Modern World

The Masai are seminomadic. They do not have permanent homes, but move across the Kenya-Tanzania border twice a year, looking for places to set up new villages. The Masai are pastoralists—people who raise livestock. The Masai raise mostly cattle. But modern forces are threatening their lifestyle. Their grazing lands have been filled up with towns, roads, and wildlife preserves. Since raising cattle has become so difficult, some Masai have turned to farming and fishing. Others earn money by selling their crafts or working in the city.

BEING MASAI

What does it mean to be Masai? The name Masai refers to people who speak the Maa language, but the Masai have a different story about who they are. They believe that Enkai, their god, made all the cattle in the world just for them. This is why they love cattle so much, even more than they love sheep and goats (*right*). In the past, Masai warriors stole cattle from other tribes. But because the Masai believed that all the world's cattle rightfully belonged to them, they did not view this action as stealing.

A LAND OF CONTRASTS

Masailand is a wide open place, where the eye can see for miles. It is a land of contrasts. Dry desert sands surround large lakes. Steep-sided valleys and gorges plunge in the middle of flat plains. Low grasslands lie next to towering volcanoes. Masailand is also the site of a clash of cultures. This clash involves the Masai, who still live much as they have for hundreds of years, and visitors from abroad, who bring with them modern tools and clothing and new ways of living.

Below: Mount Kilimanjaro peaks above the clouds. The mountaintop is very cold, even on hot summer days.

A Chain of Lakes

A string of lakes runs through Masailand. These lakes provide water for the Masai and their cattle and are home to many birds, fish, and other animals. When food supplies are low, the Masai sometimes fish in the lakes, although they are not traditionally a fishing people. Lake Turkana, a large lake in northern Kenya, has the biggest population of crocodiles in Africa. Other big lakes in East Africa include Lake Tanganyika on the western edge of Tanzania and Lake Victoria northwest of Tanzania. Lake Victoria is the second largest freshwater lake in the world. (The largest is Lake Superior in North America.)

Above: A hot spring on the western shore of Lake Bogoria

Mountains and Volcanoes

Masailand is mostly flat but is dotted with tall mountains. Most of these are volcanoes that have not erupted in a long time. Some reach thousands of feet into the sky, where the air is very cold. Snow covers their peaks, even when the weather down at ground level is hot. Mount Kilimanjaro in Tanzania is the tallest mountain in Africa. It has two peaks: Kibo is about 19,000 feet (5,791 meters) high, and Mawenzi is about 17,000 feet (5,182 meters) high. Mount Kenya, rising to more than 17,000 feet, lies near the equator, the imaginary line around the middle of the earth. There are also other, smaller mountains in East Africa.

THE GREAT RIFT VALLEY

The Great Rift Valley is a series of deep gashes in the earth. It is more than 4,000 miles (6,437 kilometers) long and cuts right through Masailand. For millions of years, volcanoes in the valley have been erupting, throwing up ash that enriches the soil. As the ash settles on the ground, the weight of the new ash layers turns the older layers into rock. As the valley widens, the old rock layers become exposed (*right*). These old layers contain fossils—remains of plants and animals that lived in the region a long time ago. Many scientists come to the Great Rift Valley to study these fossils.

THE PLANTS OF EAST AFRICA

Scientists have found thousands of different plants in East Africa, and there are probably hundreds more species yet to be discovered. These plants live in several different environments: in the Great Rift Valley, on the Serengeti Plain in northern Tanzania, along the coast of Kenya, and on the slopes of Mount Kilimanjaro and the other mountains.

Gigantic Plants

The slopes of Mount Meru in Tanzania are home to some of the world's largest plants. Perhaps because of the strong sunlight, rich volcanic soil, and steady rainfall that this mountain receives, plants tend to grow a lot bigger here than they do in other places. For example, plants called groundsels and lobelias can grow taller than people! The giant groundsel reaches up to 18 feet (5.5 meters) in height and can withstand cold weather high in the mountains.

Smaller species of the same plants are also found on the plains. The Masai use these plants to make various items they need, such as medicines.

Left: The giant groundsel

The Masai Mara

The plains where the Masai roam with their cattle herds are filled with small shrubs and trees called acacias. Acacia trees have olive green leaves and clusters of little flowers. Because so many acacia trees grow among the golden grasses, part of Masailand looks like a golden sea spotted with flecks of green. This region is called the Masai Mara. The word *mara* means "spotted" in the Maa language.

Above: The acacia tree is about the size of a mulberry tree. It has rough black bark, sharp spreading branches, and many thorns. Its olive green leaves are a tasty meal for elephants.

An Ocean of Grass

The western plains of Kenya and Tanzania are like an ocean of grass. Many wild plant-eating animals, such as wildebeests, gazelles, and zebras, spend their days chewing the grass on these plains. But the grass does not always grow in the same place at the same time. It grows only when and where rain falls, and rain patterns change during the year. When the seasons change, rain stops falling in one place, and the grass dries up. The rain shifts and begins falling in another place, feeding the grass in the new spot.

Every year, huge herds of wildebeests follow the rains in search of fresh grass. The Masai and their herds of cattle, sheep, and goats follow the wildebeests, because they trust the wild animals to find the best grass.

USEFUL PLANTS

Traditionally the Masai didn't grow or gather plants for food. But in recent years, some Masai villagers have begun planting gardens. They grow gourds called calabashes and use the shells as containers for milk and beer. They trade with farming tribes for corn, wheat, and millet, using these grains to feed themselves and their cattle when other food is scarce. The Masai also use plants that grow in the wild (*right*). For example, they use the branches of the acacia tree to build houses and fences, and they make seats and bowls out of wood from tree trunks. They weave sleeping mats out of grasses.

THE ANIMALS OF EAST AFRICA

Masailand is home to many kinds of animals. Besides the cattle, sheep, and goats that the Masai raise, there are birds, antelopes, lions, and other animals that live in the wild. In the past, the Masai used spears to kill lions and leopards that attacked their cattle. For a young Masai man, killing his first lion was a big event. In modern times, because many animals are endangered in Africa, killing wild animals has been outlawed. The Masai are not allowed to kill a lion or leopard, even if it enters their territory.

Birds

Of the world's 9,000 bird species, more than a thousand have been seen in Kenya. These include flamingos, eagles, vultures, hornbills, ducks, storks, sunbirds, sandpipers, flycatchers, egrets, herons, and owls. The Masai hunt kingfishers, orioles, bee-eaters, barbets, lovebirds, and ostriches, and make headdresses (elaborate hats) out of the stuffed birds and their feathers. The Masai wear these headdresses on special occasions.

Below: The wing feathers of an adult male ostrich can grow longer than 30 inches (76 centimeters).

Plant Eaters

More than thirty species of antelopes live in Kenya. Many of them eat grasses, but some eat the shoots and leaves of small trees. The largest antelopes are elands, which have long spiral-shaped horns. Other kinds of antelopes include impalas, gnus, hartebeests, and topis. Antelopes can run very fast, and this helps them escape predators such as lions and cheetahs. Hippopotamuses, rhinoceroses, buffalo, and elephants are some other plant-eating animals in East Africa.

Left: A mature male impala crowned with a beautiful set of full-grown horns

Above: A cheetah can run as fast as 70 miles per hour (113 kilometers per hour) over short distances.

Meat Eaters

Lions are the top predators in East Africa. They are carnivores—animals that eat meat. Lions live in large groups and often hunt in packs. Female lions do most of the hunting, because they are lighter and can run faster than the males. Cheetahs are the fastest animals on land and can easily outrun their prey over short distances. Unlike lions, cheetahs prefer to hunt alone. Sometimes a few male cheetahs hunt together. They hunt small antelopes like the Thomson's gazelle. Hyenas are scavengers—animals that feed on meat left behind by other animals. They live in packs headed by females. Hyenas usually eat food left behind by lions, cheetahs, and leopards. Occasionally, they hunt and kill animals themselves, or fight with other animals over a kill.

THE MOST IMPORTANT ANTELOPE

Wildebeests (*below*) are bearded, horned antelopes with broad shoulders and thin legs. They migrate back and forth between Kenya and Tanzania each year, always in search of fresh green grass. Wildebeests are the most important of all the antelopes to the Masai. When the huge herds of wildebeests gather together and move north or south between Kenya and Tanzania, the Masai know it is time to gather up their cattle and follow the wildebeests.

PRESERVING THE WILDLIFE

In the late 1800s and early 1900s, foreign hunters came to Africa to kill wild animals. Wealthy people bought animal head trophies and skins from the hunters and used them to decorate their homes. Other foreigners came to catch wild animals for display in zoos. Soon the animals began to die out. In recent years, the governments of Tanzania and Kenya have created preserves, areas set aside for the protection of wildlife. One example is the Meru National Park in Kenya. This space of 336 square miles (870 square kilometers) is home to elephants, giraffes, hippopotamuses, leopards, and over 300 species of birds. The Masai are not allowed to bring their cattle into these preserves. Tourists can visit the preserves to see the animals and take pictures, but they cannot hunt or hurt the animals.

Above: Early European explorers took native guides with them on their African adventures.

Above: A sign at the entrance to the Meru National Park in Kenya

A Rich Ecosystem

The Serengeti and Masai Mara wildlife preserves cover 6,400 square miles (16,576 square kilometers) of land in Tanzania and Kenya. They make up the Serengeti-Mara ecosystem. Each square mile of Serengeti-Mara land provides a home for hundreds of wild animals—more per square mile than anywhere else in the world.

Problems for the Masai

Everyone agrees that East Africa's wildlife should be protected. But the wildlife preserves in Kenya and Tanzania have made life difficult for the Masai. For hundreds of years, the Masai raised cattle among wild animals, moving with their herds wherever the wildebeests and other animals led them. But in modern times, because they cannot enter preserves to graze their cattle, the Masai cannot roam as freely as they did before. Their traditional way of life is changing.

POACHING

Poaching—the illegal hunting of wild animals—continues in East Africa (*above*), despite the creation of wildlife preserves and restrictions on hunting. In the late 1900s, poachers killed thousands of zebras, leopards, elephants, lions, cheetahs, and other animals. Some animals were killed for their meat or skins. Others were killed for their horns or tusks. The black rhinoceros has almost completely died out after years of being hunted for its horn. In Kenya, more than 10,000 elephants were killed for their tusks in the 1970s and 1980s. The Kenyan government banned the killing of elephants in 1990, and since then the elephant population has risen from 19,000 to almost 27,000. Anyone caught poaching in Kenya or Tanzania may be fined and sent to jail.

PEOPLE FROM THE NILE

The Masai did not always live in East Africa. Historians believe that their ancestors originally lived in a part of the Nile River valley, northwest of present-day Kenya. Beginning in the 1400s, historians think, the Masai left their home on the Nile and traveled down the Great Rift Valley into Tanzania. The Maa language is similar to a number of other languages spoken in the Nile region. It sounds a lot like Bari, a language spoken in present-day Sudan. Since the two languages are so much alike, historians think that the Masai and the people who speak Bari were once neighbors. Other clues to where the Masai come from—where their ancestors lived—can be found in the way they dress and behave and in their age-old customs and traditions.

Migration to Masailand

The Masai may have first left their home in the Nile region to escape a bad situation, such as drought or war with another native group. When the Masai arrived in Tanzania and Kenya, they found other native groups already living there, including the Kalenjin, Bantu, and Luo peoples. The Masai waged war on these groups, driving them out of the region. That is how the Masai earned a reputation for being fierce warriors.

Right: This wooden sculpture of a Masai family shows the way the Masai dress and the tools they use.

Left: A Bantu chief armed with a spear for hunting. Bantu peoples lived in East Africa before the first Masai arrived from the Nile region.

Above: Turkana nomads feed their hungry goats. The Turkana herd cattle in the savanna of northwestern Kenya. Like the Masai, they are facing pressure to change the way they live.

Cattle People

For the Masai, cattle herds are a sign of wealth. People occasionally give cows as wedding presents, trade cows for other items, or kill cows for funeral feasts, but they never sell cattle for money. The Maa language has more than thirty names for different kinds of cattle, depending on an animal's color and the shape of its horns. The Masai are not the only East African people who herd animals for a living. Other pastoral groups include the Jie and the Turkana.

DRESSED LIKE THE ROMANS

Wearing red togas and brown leather sandals, with their locks braided neatly in a helmetlike hairdo, and carrying shields and long spears, Masai warriors (*right*) look a lot like the ancient Roman soldiers. Roman troops occupied Egypt and other areas around the Nile River more than two thousand years ago, when the Masai still lived in the region. Because the costumes are so similar, it is possible that the Roman soldiers might have influenced the Masai warriors in their style of dress.

EARLY INHABITANTS

People have probably lived in Masailand for about two million years. Archaeologists, scientists who study past human cultures, have found some of the oldest known human bones in Olduvai Gorge in Tanzania and around Lake Turkana in Kenya. During the Stone Age, the first period in human history, people in East Africa made tools from stone. They hunted animals and gathered wild plants for food and clothing.

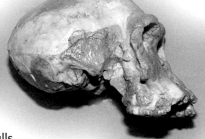

Parts of human skulls found in Olduvai Gorge

Later inhabitants of East Africa learned to make tools from metal and to raise plants and animals for food.

Finding Masailand

In ancient times, people in Egypt, Greece, Rome, and Arabia heard stories about the rich lands of East Africa. But it was difficult to visit and explore Africa, as people could travel only on foot or by horse, camel, or boat. Also there were no telephones, radios, or computers to help travelers communicate with people far away. Early explorers had a hard time reaching and mapping Africa. Since Africa seemed like such a strange land, ancient mapmakers drew it on the edge of the earth.

Early Visitors

Roman traders reached Kenya's coast about two thousand years ago. Soon after, Arabs, Persians, Indians, and Chinese traveled to the coast of Kenya to trade with the Romans.

The Portuguese explorer Vasco da Gama arrived on the coast of Kenya in 1498, around the time the Masai first left their homes in the Nile region. Later, in the 1800s, British and German traders came to Kenya and Tanzania.

Left: Vasco da Gama visited East Africa during his travels from 1497 to 1498.

Early Traders

From the early days, the Masai traded with other native peoples, exchanging goats and sheep for grain and medicine. The Masai also traded with the Portuguese, British, and German travelers who came to East Africa. The foreigners came to obtain things they could not get in their own countries, such as rhinoceros horns, leopard skins, tortoiseshell, and elephant tusks. The Masai and other native peoples who knew the land well helped the foreigners find these valuable items. In return, the outsiders gave the Masai metal cooking pots, knives, and other objects made in far-off countries. Early traders also brought beads, which the Masai used to make colorful jewelry.

Right: An early map of Africa

WHERE DOES THE NILE RIVER START?

The Nile River flows for more than 4,000 miles (6,437 kilometers), from East Africa north to the Mediterranean Sea. In ancient times, people in Egypt and Rome heard stories about a great lake in East Africa, thought to be the source of the Nile. Around A.D.150, Claudius Ptolemy, a famous Greek astronomer and geographer, drew the origin of the Nile on a map. But because the Nile region was mostly unexplored at the time, Ptolemy's map was not very accurate. Many centuries later, in the 1800s, European explorers set out to find the origin of the Nile. In 1858, an English explorer found Lake Victoria, also called Victoria Nyanza, located between Tanzania, Uganda, and Kenya. Lake Victoria is the Nile's main source.

EUROPEAN AND AFRICAN RULE

European explorers discovered that Africa was rich in natural resources. Hoping to profit from these riches, more and more Europeans came to Africa. Missionaries, religious teachers who wanted to convert the native people to Christianity, did not respect native culture and urged the native people to practice Christianity instead of their traditional customs and religions. But the missionaries also helped the native people by building schools, hospitals, and roads in many parts of Africa.

Below: A mission built by Krapf and Rebmann in Africa

Mission to Map Masailand

In 1846, two German missionaries, Johann Ludwig Krapf and Johannes Rebmann, arrived in Masailand. They were not just missionaries; they were explorers. They rode horses and camels and walked hundreds of miles, carrying compasses to guide them and tools to draw maps. In 1848, Rebmann and Krapf became the first Europeans to see Mount Kilimanjaro. Their sketches of East Africa showed the vast grasslands of Masailand and the enormous Lake Nyasa (also called Lake Malawi), which they described as an "inland sea."

Below: Joseph Thomson (*center*) was a famous Scottish explorer in Africa.

The Conquest of Africa

The powerful European nations divided Africa and its riches among themselves. In different parts of Africa, Europeans set up colonies—groups of settlers who established new rules for the territory. In the 1880s, the Germans took over Tanzania, and the British took control of Kenya. Later, in the early 1900s, the British took control of Tanzania.

The Division of Masailand

The British and Germans in East Africa set up farms and other businesses. They built towns, roads, and railroads that cut through Masai grazing lands. These changes disrupted Masai life and their harmony with the land and animals.

INDEPENDENT AFRICA

The African people longed to lead their own countries. In the early 1960s, Tanzania and Kenya won their independence from the British and set up new governments (*right*) run by Africans, not Europeans. Some Masai people took jobs with the new governments. Some became politicians. Others became game wardens in wildlife preserves. But many continued to live as cattle herders.

HOW ARE YOUR CATTLE TODAY?

Cows are the center of Masai life. To the Masai, cattle are not just wealth, but also a link to their god, Enkai. The Masai believe that they and their cattle would not exist without each other. Cows are so important that the Masai even greet one another by asking, "How are your cattle today?"

Cattle Ownership

No two cows look alike. There are black cows, white cows, and brown cows. The typical Masai elder (older man) owns about fifty cows and bulls. He identifies them by a mark branded on their hides. Each family uses a different sign carved on a small piece of metal. They heat the metal and burn the cow's hide with it. The fur does not grow back on the burned patch of skin and leaves a permanent mark on the cow.

Above: A Masai warrior herds the village cattle.

Caring for Cows

Everyone in the family—male and female, young and old—helps take care of the animals. The women and girls milk the cows twice a day and take the baby cattle indoors at night. The men and boys herd the cattle and chase away lions, leopards, and hyenas, which can kill weak or young cattle. The youngest children help feed and milk the goats.

Above: A Masai woman milks a cow.

The Most Valuable Animal

Cows are the most valuable animal to the Masai—more valuable than the sheep, goats, and donkeys in their herds. Cows give the Masai their main meal—a nutritious drink of cow's milk mixed with bull's blood. The Masai never kill a bull to get its blood. They use an arrow to lightly puncture the bull's neck, being careful not to kill it. The Masai don't usually kill cattle for food either. But if a cow or bull dies or is slaughtered for a special occasion, people will eat its meat and make its skin into clothing. They do not waste any part of the animal. The Masai also trade healthy cattle for other items.

Above: The bull's blood is collected in a gourd to be drunk pure or mixed with milk.

ON THE MOVE

During the dry season in Masailand, the rains stop falling, the weather gets hot and dry, and the food supply decreases. When the rainy season begins, a heavy down-pour waters the ground and brings new life to the dried-up plains. The rains fill up the rivers, and a new carpet of green grass grows where the grass had once been brown. This grass attracts wild herds of gazelles and wildebeests from far away. The herds travel toward the fresh green plains, and the Masai leave their villages and follow the animals. During this migration, families sleep in the wild, with the warriors guarding the cattle at night. The trip to a new spot might take several weeks. When the Masai arrive in their fresh grazing lands, they build a new village there.

TOURISM IN MASAILAND

Every year, thousands of people come to East Africa from all over the world to see Mount Kilimanjaro and the Great Rift Valley. Tourists also visit the Masai to learn about their way of life. The Masai used to pose with tourists for photographs and allow them into their villages for free. But in recent years, the Masai have become less generous with tourists and will pose for photographs only if they are paid money. Usually, tourists cannot enter a Masai village without paying a fee at the village gate.

Below: A Masai woman fits a beaded bracelet around a tourist's wrist.

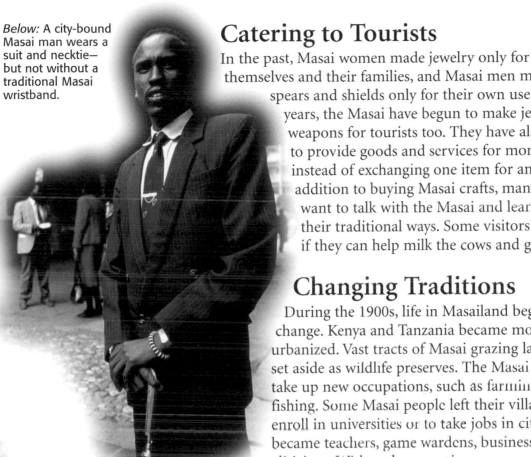

Below: A city-bound Masai man wears a suit and necktie—but not without a traditional Masai wristband.

Catering to Tourists

In the past, Masai women made jewelry only for themselves and their families, and Masai men made spears and shields only for their own use. In recent years, the Masai have begun to make jewelry and weapons for tourists too. They have also learned to provide goods and services for money, instead of exchanging one item for another. In addition to buying Masai crafts, many tourists want to talk with the Masai and learn about their traditional ways. Some visitors even ask if they can help milk the cows and goats!

Changing Traditions

During the 1900s, life in Masailand began to change. Kenya and Tanzania became modern and urbanized. Vast tracts of Masai grazing lands were set aside as wildlife preserves. The Masai began to take up new occupations, such as farming and fishing. Some Masai people left their villages to enroll in universities or to take jobs in cities. They became teachers, game wardens, businessmen, and politicians. With each generation, more and more Masai people moved to the cities.

NEW MATERIALS

Traditional Masai clothing is made from animal skins. But tourists and other foreigners have brought factory-woven cloth that the Masai use to make cloaks and capes. Many Masai people, especially in Tanzania, wear Western-style T-shirts, pants, dresses, jackets, and shoes. Foreigners have also brought watches, cameras (*right*), and new kinds of containers to Masailand. Traditionally Masai women used dried, hollowed-out calabashes as containers for collecting cow's milk. In modern times, Masai women use a variety of factory-made containers, such as tin cans. But they still use calabashes to store milk at home.

THE MASAI HOUSEHOLD

The Masai practice polygyny, meaning that each man marries more than one wife and has more than one set of children. As a result, a married man does not live in one house all the time. He regularly visits the homes of his different wives and children. Each married woman builds and owns a house, where she lives with her children. Masai houses are huts made of branches, twigs, and clay.

Above: Masai women relax with their children outside a mud-and-dung hut.

Building the Hut

To build her hut, a Masai woman mixes cattle dung and mud into a sticky clay. She uses this clay to join branches and twigs to form the walls of the hut. The clay dries quickly into a hard plaster and holds the sticks firmly together. After the first layer of clay dries, the woman applies additional layers of clay to further strengthen the walls.

The roof is made from layers of grass that block out the sun and rain so that the hut stays cool and dry inside. Masai huts have doorways but rarely have windows. The women plug any holes that develop in the walls or roof of their houses with some extra clay mixture, which they keep in a bucket.

Above: A Masai woman sticks twigs in the clay wall of her new hut.

Storing Supplies

There are no grocery stores where the Masai live, so they can't simply walk out to buy food whenever they need it. Instead, they have learned to plan and prepare for dry periods, when there is little food. The Masai store extra food supplies inside their huts—bags of grain, water in cowhide sacks, and calabash gourds filled with milk and honey beer.

Above: The interior of a Masai hut serves not just as living space but also as a storeroom for emergency supplies.

BABY BOYS, BABY GIRLS, AND BABY ANIMALS

Sometimes hungry lions sneak into Masai villages at night and kill animals. Baby animals are especially vulnerable, so the Masai bring the babies into their huts at night for protection (*right*). Masai children grow up side by side with the baby animals. The children feed the animals, take care of them, and play with them.

THE MASAI VILLAGE

A Masai village, called an *enkang*, is home to several families of the same clan. It usually contains ten to twenty huts—one for each woman in the village and her children. The small squat huts are built in a large ring, with a thornbush fence surrounding the entire village. By living so close together, the villagers can look out for one another, especially in times of danger. At night, they herd all their animals through the village gates into a pen in the middle of the ring of huts. This arrangement helps keep the animals safe from both human intruders and wild animals such as lions.

Above: A Masai village is a ring of huts surrounded by a thornbush fence.

The Fence

The fence surrounding the Masai village is usually 5 to 6 feet (1.5 to 1.8 meters) high. It is made of reeds and small straight branches, woven into a kind of barbed wire (and just as sharp). The fence gives the villagers and their animals extra protection from intruders who might try to break in and steal or kill cattle. Over time, bushes and trees grow along the fence, creating a hedge around the outside of the village. The trees provide shady gathering places, where people can meet away from the heat of the sun. The villagers sometimes plant calabash and corn near the fence.

Above: The thorn-bush fence keeps out predators and other attackers.

The Gates

The village fence is a full circle, with a number of gates that allow people to enter and exit. The Masai and their animals pass through the gates during the day, but the gates are closed tight every night to keep out unwanted guests and predators. Each married woman in the village owns not only her own hut but also her own gate in the fence. So the number of gates is equal to the number of huts in the village. This arrangement gives each woman and her children their own space and privacy.

THE PATH HOME

From each hut in the Masai village, a path leads to a gate in the fence. Outside the village fence, more paths (*right*) lead to the shade of scattered trees, the nearest lakes and rivers, and grazing lands for cattle. The grazing lands are usually green, but as the Masai and their cattle walk on the grass over and over again, their feet wear away new paths. The paths look red, because of all the red ocher in the soil of Masailand.

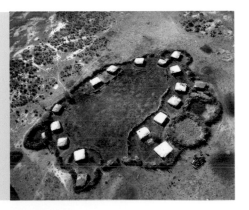

LIFE AS A MASAI CHILD

Masai society is organized into groups called age sets. Every Masai person belongs to an age set, based on his or her age and gender. As the people in each age set move from one stage of life to the next, they change their appearance and sometimes even their homes. In this way, the Masai go through all the major life stages with the same friends. This system helps the Masai build strong lasting bonds with one another.

All the Children Are Well

"All the children are well" is a Masai greeting that means that life is good and peaceful. Children are even more important to the Masai than cattle. When a Masai woman is pregnant, she eats well for her baby, and her relatives help her with her household chores. After giving birth, Masai mothers always carry their babies with them. Other family members also watch the children closely and shower them with love.

Ear Piercing

Between ages seven and eight, Masai children have their ears pierced. Both the boys and the girls wear small earrings.

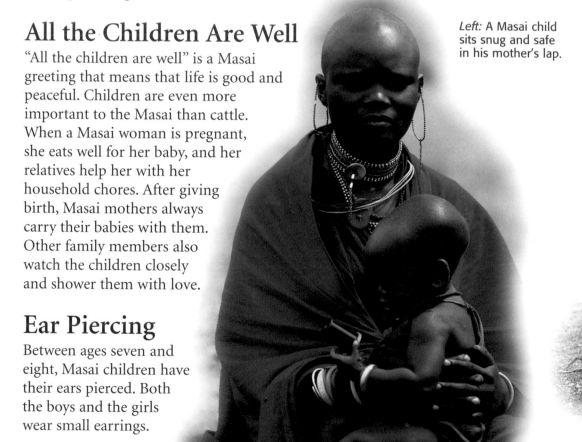

Left: A Masai child sits snug and safe in his mother's lap.

Playtime

Masai children spend a lot of time playing. The boys play around the men, and the girls play close to the women. But playtime is not all fun. It trains the children for their adult jobs. For instance, the boys play war games that prepare them to be warriors. They also help the men with the cattle in the fields.

Masai girls learn about housekeeping by helping their mothers gather sticks for building houses, cook for the family, milk the cattle, clean the house, make beaded jewelry, and sew clothes out of animal skins.

In the past, Masai children never went to school. In modern times, however, some Masai children attend schools near their villages.

Above: Some Masai boys attend school and help tend cattle in the fields.

FRIENDS FOR LIFE

The division of the Masai community into age sets makes life very neat and orderly. Each age set has its own activities and rules. Every person knows his or her role in society. Friendships grow very strong between people in the same age set (*below*), because they all eat, play, and work together year after year for as long as they live. These friendships also form important links between families. Families become so close that they readily help one another in times of need and often plan marriages between their sons and daughters.

COMING OF AGE

When Masai boys and girls become teenagers, they go through a special initiation ceremony. This is similar to coming-of-age ceremonies for young people in other cultures, such as bar mitzvah and bat mitzvah for Jewish boys and girls turning thirteen. After the coming-of-age ceremony, the child is expected to take on the responsibilities of an adult. Masai children are usually initiated between the ages of thirteen and seventeen. Everyone in the age set is initiated at once. After the initiation ceremony, Masai teenagers are recognized as men and women. The young men are ready to become junior warriors, and the young women are ready to get married.

Below: When Masai boys become warriors, they leave their home village to live in the *manyatta*, or warrior village.

From Boys to Men

The boys' initiation ceremony is called the *emorata*. After the ceremony, the new junior warriors leave their home village with their mothers and girlfriends to join the older warriors in a manyatta, a separate settlement outside the home village.

Above: Masai boys are recognized as men after their initiation ceremony.

Life in the Manyatta

For the next ten to fifteen years after initiation, a Masai warrior lives in the manyatta, eating and drinking with the other warriors. He wears a red cloak and carries a spear and a shield. He grows his hair long and smears his face and hair with oil and red ocher paint.

Masai warriors spend hours braiding their long hair and decorating themselves with beaded jewelry made by their girlfriends. The warriors lead relatively carefree lives in the manyatta, enjoying food and games and practicing their herding skills.

But when they leave the manyatta and go into the village, the warriors sometimes put their lives at great risk, doing dangerous jobs such as defending the cattle from lions.

Above: A young Masai warrior practices his spear-throwing skills in the manyatta.

WARRIORS NO MORE?

In the past, Masai warriors killed lions, stole cattle from other native groups, and sometimes fought with neighboring tribes. In modern times, these practices have generally died out. Killing lions has been outlawed in Kenya and Tanzania. Fewer and fewer Masai make their living only by raising cattle, and native groups rarely fight with one another for cattle or territory. Even so, Masai warriors (*right*) still learn cattle-raiding and fighting techniques. They still learn to defend their herds from lions and other predators. Everyone in the village admires and respects the warriors for their strength and bravery.

GIRLS BECOME WOMEN

Masai girls spend most of their time at home, helping with the household chores. Life before the initiation ceremony is simple and carefree. Girls with warrior boyfriends spend a lot of their days in the manyatta, playing with the warriors and making jewelry for them. The girls usually become very attached to the warriors but never marry them. They can only marry the elders—men who are older than the warriors and who live outside the manyatta. A Masai girl is not allowed to marry before she has been initiated. Only after her initiation ceremony will her parents choose a suitable elder to marry their daughter.

Left: A young Masai girl sits with her warrior boyfriend.

Above: A group of Masai women build a hut.

After Initiation

Life for a Masai woman centers around marriage and family. After her initiation, her parents negotiate with the elder of their choice for an agreeable bride price. This is a payment, in the form of cattle, that the elder must make to the young woman's family. If the parents accept the proposal, the elder showers the bride's family with many gifts. Preparations for the wedding begin. After the wedding, the woman builds her new home in her husband's village. She raises her children and takes care of her husband. She owns her own home and makes all the decisions concerning her household.

Before Marriage

Immediately after the initiation ceremony, Masai girls wear a special headdress that partially covers their face. This shows the men in the village that the girls are not yet ready for marriage.

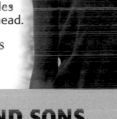
Right: A newly initiated Masai girl wears beaded tassles on her forehead.

MOTHERS AND SONS

A Masai mother participates in every major event and phase in her son's life. During the warrior years, she lives in the manyatta and cooks and cares for him. When the time comes for the son to become an elder, the mother shaves off his braids (*left*) and helps other mothers build a shelter for the ceremony. When the son marries, the mother's house serves as the site of the wedding ceremony. Afterward, the mother takes her new daughter-in-law under her roof until the young wife builds her own house. The mother will also help bring up her son and daughter-in-law's children.

MASAI ELDERS

At about age thirty, Masai warriors are ready for their next phase of life—junior elderhood. A ceremony called the *eunoto* marks the warriors' entrance into this next phase. At the ceremony, a cow is sacrificed, and the mothers of the new junior elders slice the animal's hide into thin strips. Each mother gives a ring of hide to her son as a mark of his passage into elderhood. He is now ready to marry. He will choose a prospective bride and propose marriage by showering her family with many gifts.

Right: Junior elders shed the long braids they kept while they were warriors.

Left: The senior elders hold a position of honor and respect in the Masai community.

Senior Elders

The junior elders learn from the more experienced senior elders, the oldest and wisest men in the village. The senior elders belong to a council that rules the community, makes important decisions, and resolves disputes. The senior elders speak persuasively and are good at solving problems. They teach the Masai community about religion, family history, rules of right and wrong, and medicinal plants and cures for illnesses. When the junior elders have gained enough knowledge and wisdom from their seniors, they too will become senior elders.

Accomplished Elders

The father of a junior elder is called an accomplished elder. He goes through a ceremony called the Passing of the Fence. He moves into a separate hut for four days. Then he returns home wearing a special outfit—a fur cape draped over a black calfskin cloak decorated with beads. He walks with a cane, a flywhisk, and a gourd of honey beer.

RESPECT FOR THE ELDERLY

Senior elders are respected for their age, experience, and wisdom. They spend a lot of their time in deep thought. The senior elders do not work, because the other people in the village take care of their needs, providing them with food, clothing, and housing. Older women (*right*) also have power in Masai society. They play an important role in village ceremonies, and they often gather together to bring problems to the attention of the senior elders.

ARTS, CRAFTS, AND CLOTHING

When all their other work is done for the day, Masai girls and women gather and make clothing and jewelry for themselves and their family members. These items are worn in special ceremonies. They also show the status of the wearer. For example, married women, warriors, and elders all wear different kinds of clothes and decorations. Masai artwork is not only practical, but also beautiful. In recent years, people from other cultures have developed an interest in Masai artwork.

Beaded Jewelry

From childhood through old age, the Masai decorate themselves with beaded ornaments. The women wear wide flat beaded collars. The newly initiated young women wear special headdresses with long beaded tassels covering their forehead. The warriors wear special beaded bands on their head, ears, neck, waist, and ankles.

Modern Masai women make additional jewelry and other traditional crafts to sell to tourists. They make these ornaments by threading colorful ceramic beads onto wires and using leather as backing material for the beadwork.

Right: A colorful display of traditional Masai jewelry

Right: A Masai woman making a neck coil

Other Masai Crafts

Masai women use leather to make many other useful and decorative items, such as bags, water sacks, belts, and sandals. They use the hides of different animals—cattle, sheep, and goats—to make different items. The softest kind of leather, the skin of a young goat, is used to make brides' dresses. Leatherwork requires great skill, and the women work very carefully, especially when handling the skin of cattle. Gourds are another raw material used in Masai artwork. The women paint beautiful designs on gourds used to store milk and honey beer. Some foreigners pay high prices for hand-painted Masai gourds.

Capes and Cloaks

The Masai wear different kinds of capes and cloaks, depending on their status in society. Senior elders wear fur cloaks, while the fathers of the junior elders wear fur capes over calf cloaks decorated with beads. Newly initiated young men and women wear cloaks blackened with oil and coal.

The Masai wear their cloaks in different ways. They might drape a cloak from the head, shoulders, chest, or waist. They might drape it over one or both shoulders and hold it closed with knots tied in the front or the back.

The Masai usually make their clothes out of leather, but they sometimes use commercial fabrics. Many Masai people, especially in Tanzania, have given up wearing traditional cloaks in favor of Western-style outfits.

ART FOR TOURISTS

Many Masai women earn extra money for their families by selling crafts to tourists. In past years, the women set up stalls near wildlife preserves, displaying their beaded jewelry, clothes, and decorated gourds (*below*) on posts there. Tourists visiting the preserves could browse and choose what they wanted to buy. In recent years, tour agencies have started to take visitors right to the Masai villages to buy crafts. Many foreign dealers also buy arts and crafts from the Masai to sell in other countries.

MEN'S ADORNMENTS

Depending on their status, Masai men carry different kinds of tools and wear different kinds of decorations. For instance, the warriors carry shields. Each warrior paints his shield with different designs in red, black, and white. The elders carry flywhisks (used for brushing away flies) made from the tails of wildebeests and decorated with beads.

Above: Masai shields are made of stiff cowhide stretched over oval wooden frames.

Hairdos and Headdresses

Masai warriors spend a lot of time grooming and adorning themselves to perfection. They braid their long hair into dreadlocks, which they smear with red ocher paint and oil. They decorate their heads in an array of ways. For instance, a boy going through his initiation period wears an ostrich feather on his head. Just before he is accepted as a junior warrior, he makes a headdress out of stuffed birds that he has killed in the wild. A warrior who has killed a lion gets to wear a headdress made from the lion's mane. All these headdresses make the warriors appear taller and fiercer.

Left: The lion's mane headdress is called an *olawaru*.

Body Painting

Masai men and boys decorate their faces and bodies much as they decorate their cattle. Boys decorate their faces with white netlike patterns for the initiation ceremony. Warriors paint lines in different colors and directions on their faces. They also tattoo their bodies with small patterns scratched into a layer of paint on the skin. Senior warriors attend the eunoto ceremony with their heads shaved and covered in red ocher paint.

Right: A Masai warrior with wavy leg tattoos sits with an elder.

UNIFORMITY AND CREATIVITY

Masai warriors dress the same as they have for hundreds of years. They wear red cloaks, braid their long hair in dreadlocks, and paint their skin red. Yet each warrior also expresses himself through the way he wears his cloak, the kinds of jewelry he wears, and the way he decorates his face and body. He dresses and paints himself in a style that reflects his tastes, talents, feelings, and ideas—his personality. He tries to create a look for himself that is attractive and fierce at the same time.

WORDS AND MUSIC

The Masai pass down knowledge, legends, and beliefs orally—through word of mouth. Masai legends tell about death, how the world was created, and other stories. The Masai communicate through sound and music too. They sing many songs about their cattle. Many Masai festivals involve dancing and singing. Masai warriors blow on a long wind instrument to summon the senior warriors to the eunoto, the ceremony at which the warriors become elders. The instrument is made from the horn of the greater kudu, a species of African antelope.

Below: A Masai warrior blows on a decorated kudu horn to summon the senior warriors to the eunoto ceremony.

Speakers of Maa

The name Masai means "people who speak the Maa language." Maa is spoken by several East African groups, not just the Masai. These other groups include the Samburu people of Kenya and the Arusha and Baraguyu peoples of Tanzania. Each Maa-speaking group has its own dialect—a version of the language that differs somewhat from the others. There are around twenty Maa dialects in all. The people who speak the different dialects can usually understand each other, even though some words and sounds differ from dialect to dialect. The Maa language itself has two tones—high and low. Changing a word's tone, or pitch, changes its meaning. Traditionally Maa was a spoken language with no system of writing. In recent years, people have started to write down Maa words to preserve the language.

Above: Samburu warriors differ only slightly from Masai warriors in the way they dress.

Names and Proverbs

Some places in Kenya and Tanzania have Maa names. The name of Nairobi, for instance, Kenya's capital city in the cool highlands, comes from a Maa word meaning "that which is cold." The Masai have many proverbs, or old sayings, passed down through generations. "The elephant does not get tired of its tusks" means carrying our burdens without complaining. "Teeth do not see poverty" means being able to smile despite our problems.

Right: Masai children singing. The Maa saying "The children are the bright moon" means children bring pleasure to the home.

COUNTING AND GREETING IN MAA

If you wanted to count from one to ten in Maa, you would say: *obo, are, okuni, oonguan, imiet, ile, oopishana, isiet, ooudo, tomon.* If you wanted to say hello, you would say *Na kitok! Takuenya!* to a woman or *Lo murrani! Supa!* to a man. To thank someone, people say *Ashe naleng.* To say good-bye, they say *Sere.*

ONE GOD, TWO FACES

The Masai are a spiritual people. They believe in one god, Enkai, who is said to be neither male nor female. Enkai is said also to have two sides: a black side that is kind and loving and a red side that is evil and cruel. Masai legend says that thunder is the sound of the two sides of Enkai fighting. The black side wants to give rain to the people and their cattle. The red side won't allow the rain to fall, causing the earth to dry up and the people, plants, and animals to die.

The Medicine Man

The most revered of all the Masai senior elders is the

laibon, or medicine man. He is a religious leader, prophet, and healer rolled into one. According to legend, all Masai laibons are descended from the very first laibon. Mount Kilimanjaro's two peaks, Kibo and Mawenzi, are named after Masai medicine men who lived in the 1800s.

Left: A Masai laibon sitting with British officials in 1897. As the spiritual leader of the Masai, the laibon could serve as a spokesman with foreigners.

Three Kinds of Medicine Men

Traditionally there were three kinds of Masai medicine men. One practiced his craft only in private, somewhat like a family doctor. Another prayed for requests made by small groups—people asking Enkai for success in war or for more rain, for example. The third type of laibon handled general affairs for the community. He directed ceremonies and sacrifices. He led rituals and prayers. He advised the other senior elders on spiritual matters.

Death and Funerals

The Masai believe that every person has a guardian spirit. At the moment of death, this spirit carries the person to one of two places: to a desert if the person has led an evil life or to a cattle-rich land if the person has led a good life. But the Masai never say that anyone is dead. If a young person dies, he or she is said to be missing. If an old person dies, he or she is said to be sleeping.

The Masai generally do not bury their dead. They avoid digging the ground, because it is sacred to them—the earth is the source of grass for their cattle. Instead, the Masai leave dead bodies on the grassy plains, where hyenas and other scavengers eat the remains.

Right: A picture of a Masai cow painted on rock

THE LEGEND OF THE FIRST LAIBON

According to Masai legend, two warriors from different clans came upon a little boy one day. The warrior from the *il-molelian* clan decided to leave the boy alone. But the other warrior, from the *il-aiser* clan, took the boy home with him. The boy turned out to have special powers. When he took the cattle out in the dry season, rain fell, grass grew, and the cattle could eat. The boy grew up to become the first laibon in Masailand, and every laibon since has come from the il-aiser clan.

CELEBRATIONS AND CEREMONIES

At Masai ceremonies, laibons lead the villagers in prayer. Sometimes the worshipers enter a trance —a strange state in which they seem to lose touch with reality. The Masai may ask Enkai for fair and merciful treatment or for special favors. In return, they kill a bull or cow and offer it as a sacrifice to Enkai.

The Eunoto

At the eunoto, the senior warriors in the community become junior elders who are ready for marriage. Before the ceremony, each senior warrior's mother cuts off his long braids. His bald head is then smeared with red ocher paint. For four days, everyone in the village gathers to celebrate around a special hut built just for the occasion. Inside the hut, the laibon slaughters a black cow, fattened with honey beer and herbal mixtures. Blood is drawn from the cow's neck and mixed with milk for each warrior to drink. No part of the animal is wasted. The meat is roasted for a feast, and the hide is sliced into strips, which the mothers give to their junior elder sons as a mark of their graduation from their former lives as warriors. At the end of the ceremony, the senior elders bless the junior elders by blowing milk over them.

Left: A Masai mother gives her son a ring of hide at the eunoto.

Dancing

The Masai love to dance, especially at festival time. To them, dance is both a form of expression and a spiritual ritual. For instance, during the Masai fertility dance, the women ask Enkai to grant them many babies. A very popular Masai dance is the *adumu*. Standing in a circle, a group of warriors sings a rhythmic song. Then one or two of the warriors will enter the circle and begin jumping up and down in the middle. The challenge for the jumping dancers is to keep their bodies straight and their minds focused.

The Emorata

The emorata ceremony is one of the most important Masai festivals. It marks the coming of age of Masai boys.

Planning for this ceremony takes two months. First the boys give away everything they own. They will not take any old belongings into their new lives as men. Villagers collect honey to make honey beer for the elders who will attend the ceremony. They gather ostrich feathers to make special headdresses for the boys.

On the day of the ceremony, the boys shave their heads and paint their faces with white chalk. They put on black cloaks and ostrich feather headdresses. Then the village elders perform the initiation rights on each boy inside a small tent.

Right: Masai boys leaving the tent of initiation have entered the warrior phase of their lives.

A TIME OF JOY AND SORROW

Marriage is a time of both happiness and sadness for young Masai women and their families. On the day of her wedding, a Masai bride puts on a dress of the softest animal skin and prepares to leave home. She cries as she says good-bye to her family, because she will never live in her childhood village again. The groom then takes her to his mother's home. There, the women in the groom's family welcome the bride with gifts. The bride and groom enter the house, and the wedding takes place. From then on, the bride lives in her husband's village.

GLOSSARY

adumu (ah-DOO-moo): an African jumping dance

age set: a group of people of roughly the same age. All Masai people belong to an age set and move through each stage of life with this group.

clan: a group of people tracing descent from a common ancestor

colony: a settlement occupied and ruled by a foreign nation

ecosystem: an environment in which a group of plants and animals depend on and interact with one another.

emorata (ehm-mohr-AH-tah): the Masai warrior initiation ceremony

fossil: the remains of a plant or animal that lived thousands or millions of years ago

manyatta (mahn-YAH-tah): a Masai warrior settlement

migrate: to move from one region to another, often in search of fresh food sources

missionary: a religious teacher who travels to distant places to convert others to his or her own faith

ocher: a mineral ranging in color from pale yellow to orange and red

pastoralist: a person who makes a living by raising livestock

poaching: the illegal hunting of animals for trade

polygyny: the practice of having more than one wife

predator: an animal that hunts other animals for food

sacrifice: the killing of an animal or person as an offering to a god

scavenger: an animal that feeds on the leftovers from another animal's meal

seminomadic: moving from place to place sometimes and living a settled life at other times

volcano: an opening in the earth's surface through which lava, hot gases, and ashes periodically burst forth. Most volcanoes are cone-shaped mountains.

vulnerable: defenseless; easily hurt

wildlife preserve: a tract of wilderness set aside to protect the plants and animals that live there. Hunting is not allowed in preserves.

FINDING OUT MORE

Books

Aardema, Verna, and Leo Dillon (illustrator). *Who's in Rabbit's House? A Masai Tale.* New York: Dial Books for Young Readers, 1992.

Hetfield, Jamie, and Marianne Johnston. *The Maasai of East Africa (Celebrating the Peoples and Civilizations of Africa).* Logan, IA: Powerkids Press, 1997.

Hru, Dakari, and Anna Rich (illustrator). *Joshua's Masai Mask.* New York: Lee & Low, 1996.

Insight Guide to Kenya. London: APA Communications, 2000.

Kroll, Virginia, and Nancy Carpenter (illustrator). *Masai and I.* New York: Four Winds Press, 1992.

Lilly, Melinda, and Charles Reasoner (illustrator). *Warrior Son of a Warrior Son: A Masai Legend.* Mahwah, New Jersey: Troll Communications, 1998.

Videos

Beyond the Plains. Villon Films, 1982.

New Explorers: Secrets of an Ancient Culture. A&E Television Networks.

Websites

<http://website.lineone.net/~yamaguchi/culture/kencult.html>

<http://www.care.org/info_center/newsroom/1998/bride.html>

<http://www.kent.wednet.edu/curriculum/soc_studies/kenya/masai/masai.html>

<http://www.uoregon.edu/~dlpayne/maasai/madict.htm>

Organizations

Maasai Education Discovery
P.O. Box 381066
Cambridge, MA 02238
Tel: (617) 779-0619
E-mail: <info@maasaieducation.org>

Maasai Environmental Resource Coalition International Office
2020 Pennsylvania Ave. NW, Suite 136
Washington, D.C. 20006
Tel: (202) 785-8787
Fax: (202) 785-1557
E-mail: <mercmaasai@aol.com>
Website: <http://www.cs.org/specialprojects/maasai/maasai.htm>

INDEX

ABOUT THE AUTHOR

Archaeologist, anthropologist, and author Lisa McQuail has done fieldwork in central Thailand and written a book entitled *Treasures of Two Nations: Thai Royal Gifts to the United States of America*. Lisa is advertising manager and assistant editor at the American Anthropological Association.

PICTURE CREDITS

(B=bottom; C=center; I=inset; L=left; M=main; R=right; T=top)

Camerapix: 5R, 13T, 18–19M, 19T, 20–21M, 21R, 25R, 26–27M, 27I, 30–31M, 31I, 32, 33T, 33R, 33I, 34, 35T, 35I, 37T, 37I, 40–41M, 41T, 42–43M, 42B, 44B • Camera Press: 19I • Dave G. Houser/Houserstock: 31T, 45R • HBL Network Photo Agency: 44–45M • Hulton Getty/ Archive Photos: 12R, 14L • Images of Africa Photobank: 6–7M, 8–9M, 12–13M, 21T, 25I • International Photobank: 36–37M, 39T • Michele Burgess: 24–25M, 41B • Nik Wheeler: 4–5M, 15I, 25T, 28B, 29I, 43R • North Wind Picture Archives: 17T, 17R • Photobank Photolibrary/Singapore: cover • The Hutchison Library: 23T • Travel Ink Photo Library: 7T, 11I • Trip Photo Library: title page, 7I, 9I, 11L, 11T, 10–11M, 14R, 22–23M, 23I, 28–29M, 31R, 38–39M, 39R • Victor Englebert: 9L, 14–15M • William F. Wheeler/Houserstock: 27T